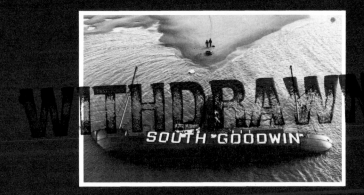

shipwreck!

Ian Dear
wreck!

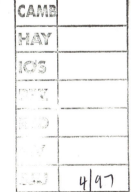

Portman Books. London

To Christopher

© Ian Dear 1990
First published 1990

All rights reserved. No parts of this publication may be reproduced, in any form or by any means, without permission from the Publisher

ISBN 0 7134 5953 0

Typeset by Tradespools Ltd., Frome, Somerset
and printed in Great Britain by
Courier International, Tiptree, Essex

This edition published 1990 by
Portman Books an imprint of
B.T. Batsford Ltd
4 Fitzhardinge Street
London W1H 0AH

Foreword

Each year about 150 merchant ships founder or are so badly damaged that they are not worth repairing. These accidents amount to more that 1,200,000 gross tons of lost shipping. Worse still, to this horrendous statistic must be added a considerable loss of life. In 1987 the death toll from shipping accidents was the highest ever recorded since records began.

It is the purpose of this book to try and focus attention on why such losses continue to occur and to show pictorially a small sample of the different types of maritime disasters that have occurred off the coast of the British Isles or in adjacent waters during the last hundred years or so. It is to be hoped that these photographs drive home the unpalatable fact that shipwrecks not only used to be a frequent occurrence but, relatively speaking, still are.

Many maritime disasters occur on the high seas with no one to witness the tragedy, Often a brief SOS or 'Mayday' is the only information the world receives on what has occurred. Occasionally, as with the *Derbyshire* in 1980, there is not even that. However, where there have been survivors or eye-witnesses, shipwrecks have been recorded since the earliest times, first in drawings, paintings, and dramatic descriptions – the bibliography of shipwrecks is substantial – and, more recently, with photographs and investigative journalism.

The post-nuclear, microchip age, besides dangerously insulating seamen from the hazards of the sea, has introduced new types of vessels to the shipping lanes around our coast lines. Hovercraft, jet foils, oil rigs, super-tankers, and the vastly expanding numbers of yachts, have all brought a new dimension to disasters at sea. For example, in March 1988 the North Sea exploration rig, *Santa Fe 135*, broke loose from its tow in 70mph (113kmph) winds 140 miles (225km) east of Aberdeen, and 44 of its crew were lifted off by helicopter. Luckily, there was no loss of life but the rig drifted so close to the Cod oil platform in the Oula field that the 39 men on that platform also had to be air-lifted to safety before tugs were able to get lines aboard the *Santa Fe*. As the loss of the oil rig *Orion* shows (see fig. 81), this type of accident is not unique, and it does not need much imagination to envisage a scenario involving one where there could not only be severe loss of life but horrendous pollution of the marine environment as well. The destruction of the North Sea oil rig, *Piper Alpha*, in July 1988, with the loss of 167 men, was not the result of a ship colliding with it. However, it is not beyond the bounds of possibility that such a serious accident could be caused by collision – such an accident was narrowly averted only four months earlier, when the abandoned hull of a ro-ro ferry, *Vinca Gorthon*, drifted perilously close to North Sea oil rigs in the Bravo field. As it was, the hull broke an oil line when it grounded off the Dutch coast, causing oil to leak into the sea.

The scene of a disaster, whether it is on a motorway or at sea, is always dramatic and sometimes overwhelmingly dreadful. Yet the photographs of maritime disasters in the book include some which have an awesome beauty of their own, a quality of stillness that is just as dramatic as the storm-tossed victim caught in other shots. They are spread round the British Isles, though not evenly, for notorious areas such as the Scillies have been the cause of far more shipwrecks than other parts of the coast line, and this seems as true today as it was a century ago. The lifeboatmen who have to cope with these disasters around our coastline are no more exempt from tragedy today than they have been in the past as the losses of the Fraserburgh (see fig. 71) and Penlee (see fig. 91) lifeboats show. These brave men – who are sometimes called upon to risk, and sometimes lose, their lives through the sheer bad seamanship of those who require their aid – should be remembered for their invaluable work. So should be the equally courageous helicopter crews who conduct air-sea rescue operations around the coasts of the British Isles, often in the most atrocious weather conditions. A number of the photographs included in this book originate from the Royal National Lifeboat Institute, and from air-sea rescue stations, and bear witness to the hazardous nature of their work.

The loss of a vessel, especially if there is also loss of life, is always tragic, but some of these photographs – particularly the modern ones – also record other types of disaster, like the horrendous pollution spread by the sinking of the *Torrey Canyon* (see fig. 72) in 1967 and the *Amoco Cadiz* (see fig. 84) in 1978. Not, every maritime accident has to be of Titanic proportions for inclusion here. Sometimes the stranding and subsequent loss of a ship is enough to justify its inclusion, But, whatever the direct cause of a vessel being in distress, these photographs bear witness to the fact that even in these days of computerization and technical perfection, the sea is an environment demanding respect and constant vigilance.

Shipwreck!

Introduction

The sinking of the Philippine ferry *Doña Paz* at the end of 1987 with the loss of over 3000 lives and the capsize of the *Herald of Free Enterprise* just outside Zeebrugge harbour a few months earlier, with the loss of 193 lives (see fig. 98/99), once again put the subject of maritime disasters into the headlines, along with the perennial question of why they continue to occur.

THE EARLIEST SHIPWRECKS

Ever since man took to travelling across water there have been shipwrecks. One of the earliest recorded, according to Kenneth Hudson in his *Book of Shipwrecks*, was estimated to have taken place around 2500 BC off the Greek island of Hydra where 20 other sunken ships from classical times have already been located.

The main causes of maritime disasters in those far-off classical times were almost certainly more or less the same as those that afflicted seamen throughout the succeeding centuries: bad design, bad weather, a hostile shore, fire, accidental damage, collision and human error. They are causes from which no type of vessel, whether freighter or passenger liner, sailing yacht or fishing trawler, has ever been immune, though some types of accident have become less prevalent. Not nearly as much used to be understood about ship design as is known nowadays, for instance, and therefore design errors are less common now – though, as we shall see, they still happen.

The development of navigational equipment

The development and refinement of navigational instruments and charts over the centuries has also lessened the number of shipwrecks caused by navigational errors. But they have not been eliminated, and an unfortunate corollary to the introduction of aids like radar has been the development of an undesirable reliance on them. The introduction, too, of a proper buoyage system, and of lighthouses and lightships, has, reduced the odds in favour of today's seamen – though, again, the modern era is far from perfect in this respect as a series of disastrous collisions (see *Texaco Caribbean* fig. 74), in the English Channel in 1971 shows.

Ironically, there is a move afoot to remove many of the more expensive visual aids to navigation around the United Kingdom on the cost-cutting pretext that in these days of electronic aids they are no longer necessary. In November 1987 *The Times* printed an article on the controversy surrounding this proposal which cast some doubt on it. It described how the Captain of a Danish-run ship, loaded with chemicals and equipped with the most sophisticated electronic navigational aides, complained to Trinity House, the lighthouse authority, that a light buoy off the Sussex coast was out of position by 1 1/2 miles (2 1/2 km). When the complaint was investigated it was found that it was the ship that had been out of position not 'the buoy'.

Natural disasters

The weather, too, is less of a hazard than it used to be at the beginning of the era covered photographically in this book, and there's little doubt that, despite the heavy loss of early steamers, the change from sail to engines as the means of getting from A to B has enormously increased safety at sea. One has only to look at the early records of shipwrecks and sinkings to realize just how hazardous a seaman's life under sail was and it is relevant to note here that few of the great square riggers which remained afloat into the age of steam survived for long. The *Preussen* (see fig. 41); *Herzogin Cecilie* (see fig. 60); *Thomas T. Lawson*, the largest sailing ship ever built; and the *Admiral Karpfanger*, the *København* and the *Pamir* all came to untimely ends, the last three with heavy loss of life. The fate of these ships underlined the fact that in extreme conditions sailing vessels, however large, were very vulnerable, and still are, as the tragic loss of life during the 1979 Fastnet Race (see fig. 89) shows.

But nowadays the loss of a modern merchant ship solely through bad sea conditions is rare for these vessels are designed to survive even the worst weather. Freak conditions can contribute to the loss of a ship – as they did when the Philippine ferry, the *Doña Marilyn*, went down with the loss of over 300 lives during Typhoon Ruby in October 1988 – but rarely, if ever, are they the sole cause of it foundering – poor maintenance, bad manning, poor judgement, uneven loading, or structural failure are invariably behind such tragedies.

Vanished without trace

Sometimes courts of enquiry are able to find the probable reason for the loss of a ship at sea, even when it vanishes without trace. When the 5880-ton oil tanker, *La Crescenta*, disappeared in November 1934 en route to Osaka from California, the court of enquiry established that she was overloaded at the time and that she was not in a seaworthy condition. *Millpool* which went down with all hands in an Atlantic storm in 1933, was likewise found to have been unseaworthy.

The crews of both these ships were victims of the Great Depression, during which many shipowners ran their vessels with an inadequate safety margin in order to squeeze some profit by keeping them running. Unfortunately, this is a problem which an improved economic climate has failed to abolish. Ships are still being lost because they are basically unfit to go to sea; and despite the improvements in design, technology and radio communications, the disappearance of large, well-found vessels continues to occur.

In September 1980 the 160,000-ton bulk carrier, *Derbyshire*, was en route from Canada to Japan when she encountered a typhoon codenamed Orchid. The force 12 winds whipped up 30-ft waves, but the *Derbyshire* was a modern ship which should have been able to ride out the most severe conditions. Yet she disappeared at the height of the typhoon and – apart from oil bubbling to the surface and a lifeboat which might have belonged to her – no trace of her was ever found. A similar disaster occurred in June 1985 when the 69,389-ton bulk carrier, *Arctic Career*, disappeared with all hands north of Tristan da Cunha. Neither had time to make a Mayday call, but, as will be seen, in both cases there were indications that the ships were structurally unsound, though there was no proof of this.

The threat of fire

In fact certain types of marine accidents continue to occur with alarming frequency. Fire, for example, remains a danger and passenger liners in particular have always been vulnerable to it, nearly 850 of them having been destroyed in this manner since the beginning of the century, sometimes with heavy loss of life. The 1920s and 1930s were expecially bad decades in this respect, and French liners were particularly vulnerable with the 10,015-ton *Fontainebleu* (1926), the 12,989-ton *Paul Lecat* (1928), the 6,122-ton *Asia* (1930), the 17,539-ton *Georges Philippar* (1930), the 45,512-ton *L'Atlantique* (1933 see fig. 59), the 25,178-ton *Lafayette* (1938) and the 34,569-ton *Paris* (1939) all being destroyed by fire, with sabotage on several occasions suspected. Fires broke out aboard two more, the beautiful

79,300-ton *Normandie* and the *Empress of Canada*, but they were ultimately destroyed by the amount of water pumped aboard them causing both to capsize. One of the worst disasters from fire occurred on 8 September 1934 when the New York & Cuba Mail Steamship Company's 11,520-ton liner, *Morro Castle*, went up in flames in the early hours of the morning off the New Jersey coast. In the panic that followed orders to abandon ship 137 lives were lost.

In more recent times fire destroyed no less than 17 passenger ships during the 1970s, including – in terms of passenger tonnage – the largest maritime disaster ever when the 83,673-ton *Seawise University* (ex *Queen Elizabeth*) went up in flames in Hong Kong harbour in 1972. Loss of life only occurred in a few of these more recent incidents, but 24 people were killed when the 11,674-ton car ferry *Heleanna* was set on fire off Brindisi in August 1971 after a gas cylinder exploded in the ship's galley, and 100 went down with the 3,920-ton *Patra* after a gas leak in the engine room set her ablaze.

Collision

Collision has also remained a constant hazard, and ships of all types continue to be victims of this, often fatal, type of accident. One of the worst passenger accidents to occur in British waters happened on the River Thames in September 1878 before adequate collision regulations had been drawn up and enforced. The excursion paddle steamer *Princess Alice* (see fig. 6), crowded with holidaymakers, was rammed by the screw steamer. *Bywell Castle*, near Woolwich with the loss of 640 lives. Even now the collision regulations on the busy Thames would appear to be inadequate, as the tragedy of the *Marchioness* (see fig. 100), run down by a much larger vessel near Southwark Bridge on 20 August 1989, shows. Other recent examples show that the problem has not lessened with time. When the Russian Black Sea cruise ship *Admiral Nakhimov*, was rammed by a Russian bulk carrier, she sank in 15 minutes with the loss of 423 lives, whilst the sinking of the Greek cruise ship, *Jupiter*, by an Italian freighter outside Piraeus harbour in October 1988, resulted in four deaths.

The loss of the grossly overloaded Philippine ferry, *Doña Paz*, in December 1987, which caused 3132 deaths, was also caused by a collision. It now ranks as the world's worst maritime disaster, an unenviable record long held by the *Titanic* (see fig. 44) and nearly repeated in June 1989, when a Soviet cruise liner *Maxim Gorky* with 952 people aboard, hit an iceberg near Spitzbergen. These tragedies serve to emphasize one of the contentions of this book – that it is essential for governments to enforce their maritime regulations, which include those governing the number of passengers aboard. And lest anyone think that overloading ferries is a Third-World practice, they should be reminded that in 1987 a British ferry had to return to France after it was found to have too many passengers....

Incidentally, it might be thought that the *Titanic* disaster could not happen nowadays – that modern equipment like radar would give a ship ample warning of any danger that lay in her path. Unfortunately, disasters that have occurred since the Second World War do not support such optimism. For example, both the 29,000-ton Italian liner, *Andrea Doria*, and the 12,644-ton Swedish American Line, liner *Stockholm*, had modern radar sets in operation off the Nantucket Lightship in July 1956. Yet they still collided in thick fog at a combined speed of 40 knots with the loss of 47 lives. Radars are much improved since this tragedy, but there are still accidents at sea which are known as radar induced collisions.

Human error

The introduction of modern navigational aids has, as mentioned, led to too much reliance being placed on them and not enough, if any, on basic seamanship and common sense. A good example of how this could lead to disaster was the case of the *Christos Bitas* (see fig. 83), an oil tanker employed by BP to run oil from Rotterdam to Belfast whose officers only used radar for position finding. On 12 October 1978, in worsening visibility in the Irish Sea, the radar broke down. The tidal streams were apparently ignored, no soundings or radio direction-finder bearings were taken, nor was any use made of the LORAN set which was aboard, and the tanker eventually ran on to the Hats and Barrels rocks off the Pembrokeshire coast. She managed to get clear of them but began leaking her cargo, threatening massive oil pollution to Cardigan Bay. Luckily, the oil was able to be transferred, and the ship was subsequently towed into the Atlantic and sunk.

Incompetence on this scale is by no means uncommon. Two ships, one carrying nearly 200,000 tons of crude oil, ran into the Bermuda Great Reef in 1984 within six weeks of each other. Both sighted Bermuda in calm weather in broad daylight, and both hit the reef at full speed. It transpired that both vessels were using satellite navigation equipment and plotting charts which did not show Bermuda at all. In fact, neither had a chart of the island, and no one on board either ship knew a reef surrounded it.

Then there is the case of the Greek owned *Aeolian Sky*, which took the wrong channel in the traffic separation scheme in the English Channel – presumably because she had out-of-date charts on board – collided with another ship, and sunk with her cargo, part of which was dangerous chemicals, still aboard.

In truth, the root cause of the loss of nearly all the ships so far mentioned is human error, a factor which even the most sophisticated equipment cannot counter. Sometimes, however, the tragedy is not caused by those on board, but by the mistakes and omissions of those who designed or were responsible for running the vessel.

Design deficiencies in ro-ro ferries

As long ago as 1967, K.C. Barnaby pointed out in his book, *Some Ship Disasters and Their Causes*, the basic flaw in the design of car ferries is where a large space, not partitioned off by bulkheads, is positioned near the water line. If the doors leading to this car space are breached by heavy seas, as occurred with the loss of the ferry, *Princess Victoria*, in the Irish Sea in 1953, or if they are left open, as happened with the *Herald of Free Enterprise*, then disaster is almost certain to follow.

Accidents with roll-on, roll-off ferries, ro-ros as they are colloquially called, are in fact distressingly frequent, and the *Herald of Free Enterprise* was not the first one to founder because of an ingress of water through her watertight doors. During a storm in the North Sea in November 1977 the 4,492-ton ro-ro vessel, *Hero* (see fig. 82), began taking in water through her stern doors and through a watertight door which had been left open in the bows. When the water could not be stemmed the crew abandoned ship and one crewman was lost. The *Hero* sank the next day.

Another ro-ro ferry, *European Gateway*, was lost off Harwich with the loss of six lives in 1982 (see Fig. 96). She, too, sank when her car deck was flooded, though on this occasion the flooding was caused by collision which was how another ro-ro ferry, the French flag *Mont Louis* (see fig. 95), was also lost in August 1985. (Even more disturbing in the case was that she was carrying a radioactive cargo.) Then in April 1986 the Philippine ro-ro vessel, *Dona Josefina*, capsized in calm weather, drowning 192 people aboard; and in March 1988 the crew of the 18,773-ton Swedish ro-ro ferry, *Vinca Gorthon*, was rescued by helicopter just before the vessel turned upside down in force-10 winds in the North Sea.

The Royal Institution of Naval Architects has now condemned ro-ro vessels as being 'unacceptably vulnerable' under certain conditions, particularly rapid capsize after a collision, and has recommended that both new and existing vessels should be fitted with transverse bulkheads on their vehicle decks that could be raised or lowered as required. The speed at which a ro-ro vessel can sink after an accident also caused the Institution concern. Conventional ships could be expected to stay upright for as long as 30 minutes when disabled; ro-ro vessels can capsize within three minutes, making escape impossible. It therefore recommended that protective sponsons or bulges be fitted to the hull and that spaces should be filled with buoyant material.

Deficiencies in conventional design

Ships of conventional design can also suffer from structural and design deficiencies. Merchant ships are designed and built to standards laid down by various classification societies, of which Lloyds is only one. Although designated 'in class' – fit for service and insurance – ships' hulls are vulnerable to rust and can deteriorate rapidly. The mild steel with which they are built is exposed not only to salt air and water from the outside but by a variety of corrosive cargoes – coal, sulphur, salt, oil – from the inside, and unless rigorously maintained to the highest standard a hull can become seriously wasted within 15 years. Add to this the modern practice of loading high density cargo like iron ore in alternate holds, and of maintaining speed in heavy weather in order to keep to a tight schedule, and it can be seen that while a new ship can withstand such a combination of stresses an old one sometimes cannot, as the disappearance of the *Arctic Career* mentioned on p. 8 illustrates.

In June 1985 this 20-year-old, 28,413-ton bulk carrier set out from Tubarao in Brazil for Indonesia loaded with iron ore. Somewhere north of Tristan da Cunha the Master reported that a bulkhead had buckled, and that a hatch coaming and some shell plates had become indented, almost certainly a sign of structural failure. The weather in the South Atlantic presents no problem to a seaworthy ship, yet the *Arctic Career* abruptly disappeared. So sudden was the disaster that no distress signal was ever received and no trace of the crew of 256 or their lifeboats was ever found.

Some of the relatives of the 44 who lost their lives aboard the ill-fated *Derbyshire* argued that for a ship of that size to go down so quickly – so quickly that there was not even time to send a Mayday – could only mean severe structural failure. The Department of Transport held two informal enquires into her loss but decided against a formal public enquiry because there was no direct evidence of what had happened. However, when a sister ship, the *Kowloon Bridge*, put into Bantry Bay in 1986 because of cracks in her hull – she subsequently sank after grounding – the Department changed its mind. A public enquiry was started in October 1987, and although this revealed that five other carriers of the same class had also experienced fractures and other faults just forward of the bridge it decided that there was no evidence to suggest that this had happened to the *Derbyshire*.

In fact, the loss of bulk carriers through various causes can be said to have reached scandalous proportions. No less that 151 bulk carriers and ore carriers were lost between September 1980 and August 1987, 38 of which foundered at sea. Eleven of these went down between January 1986 and June 1987, sometimes with heavy loss of life (see Table).

Apart from the *De Bao*, which sank on her maiden voyage after reporting water in her engine room, all these carriers were over 13 years old and three of them were 19 years old or more when they foundered. The question has been raised as to whether they were in fact fit to go to sea with cargoes of ore or scrap metal. The most recent example of a tanker suffering structural failure was when holes appeared in the plating of the 85,180 dwt carrier *Yarrawonga* after being caught in an Atlantic storm in January 1989. Luckily her 32-strong crew were all rescued by helicopter without any loss of life.

Vessel	Weight (Gross Tons)	Date of Sinking
Riviera Sky	30,371	12 Jan 1986
Luchana	8.250	15 Jan 1986
De Bao	3.995	24 Jan 1986
Brave Themis	9.324	19 Dec 1986
Cathay Seatrade	30,027	13 Jan 1987
Testarossa	66,903	14 Jan 1987
Tina	13,196	11 Feb 1987
Skipper I	14,474	30 Apr 1987
Cumberlande	21,384	12 Jun 1987
Dayspring	13,373	23 Jun 1987
Star Carrier	15,993	25 Jun 1987

Oil tankers

The record for oil tankers is equally frightening, explosions and grounding of loaded vessels wreaking havoc equally upon humanity and nature. The pollution disasters caused by the *Torrey Canyon* and *Amoco Cadiz* are well known, but neither could be compared with the environmental catastrophe caused by the *Exxon Valdez* which spilled 11 million gallons of crude oil into Prince William Sound, Alaska, after running aground on 24 March 1989. Though the above three disasters hit the headlines they are by no means isolated examples. On 5 May 1970 a 50,000-ton Norwegian oil tanker, the *Polycommander*, ran aground in the Bay of Vigo and burst into flames. The burning oil created a blanket of black, oily rain which fell over a large area, damaging crops and killing livestock.

Losses of oil tankers from fire and explosion are alarmingly frequent. Recent casualties include the 121,430-deadweight tonne oil tanker *Betelguese* (see fig. 87), which blew up in January 1979 in Bantry Bay with the loss of 50 lives; the 271,000-ton super tanker, *Castillo de Bellver*, which sank in the South Atlantic in August 1983, spilling 250,000 tons of crude oil into the sea; and the 29,990-ton *Petragon I*, which exploded in Gibraltar Bay in May 1985. (The destruction of the *Petragon I* allegedly triggered an explosion aboard a smaller tanker which was unloading aviation fuel in the next berth, and 30 lives were lost.) In all these cases empty tanks or ullages (the space left in a hold after the cargo has been loaded) had not been filled with an inert gas (diesel exhaust or nitrogen) that prevents an explosion occurring), though inert gas systems are a requirement of the International Convention for the Safety of Life at Sea that has been ratified by 100 countries.

These disasters underline the opinion of one marine writer, Douglas Foy, that most modern marine accidents are directly due to uncorrected deterioration in the ships, irresponsible officer manning and unsafe operating practices and that merchant shipping worldwide is responsible for wholesale loss of life, wholesale destruction of property and the threat of wholesale coastal pollution simply because it is so badly regulated. These remarks are no exaggeration for in recent years, on average, three ships of 500 gross registered tonnage or over have been lost *every week* by grounding, foundering at sea or explosions and marine insurance claims worldwide have been estimated to run to $300 million every month. Shipping losses for 1988 were 147 ships (775,856 gross tons) which is slightly down on 1987 in terms of tonnage (1,178,000) but up in terms of ships (139).

Owners' responsibilities

Despite these high losses it is very hard to get at the facts. Unless there is a public enquiry, owners are not required to reveal details of a loss, and the insurers will not do so either for fear of claims from cargo owners. On the other hand ship owners do not necessarily have much interest in curbing shipping losses. Hull and freight insurance is easy to obtain and the owners rarely lose out financially. Sometimes, indeed, after a loss they recoup more than their vessel could possibly be worth on the open market, and there seems little doubt that the use of unseaworthy vessels, especially when carrying high density cargoes, is a factor which contributes to the current statistics of marine fatalities. Classification societies, which might be thought to be in a position to stop unseaworthy ships going to sea, are in a difficult situation, for they are in competition with one another and are, in any case, dominated by ship owners. If an owner cannot obtain a certificate from one society he is quite entitled to get one from another which is not as fussy. A number of European countries operate a Port State Control system which involves government surveyors inspecting a certain percentage of foreign vessels, but this is a recent innovation and is designed ultimately to cover only 25 per cent of shipping entering the ports concerned.

Most of the world's maritime powers, of which Britain is still one, introduced stringent regulations to govern the seaworthiness of ships long ago, but no ship owner is obliged to fly the flag of the nation to which he belongs; he is quite entitled to register his ship in a country where the laws are often more lax and fly what is known as a 'flag of convenience'.

Inexperienced crews

These owners often employ inexperienced seamen to sail unseaworthy vessels. The profit motive drives both ship and crew to the edge of disaster, and sometimes beyond it. Where time is always of the essence, short cuts are too often taken in maintenance, repairs, correct complement of crew, even in the route taken (see *Torrey Canyon* fig. 72) and dubious loading practices and unwise navigational procedures are often followed. One experienced Master Mariner commented in a newspaper article recently:

Anything goes! Shake the nearest tree for a crew. Inexperienced and unqualified officers are common. I've sailed with a second Mate who only had one year's experience as a deckhand and was in sole charge of his watch. A Master I was with didn't understand the basic collision regulations; a later command of his was written off on the rocks near the Channel Islands. A first Mate had to be taught how to plot radar targets when we hit dense fog. All were serving in big flag of convenience (f-o-c) ships.

A prime example of a disaster being precipitated by inexperienced officers is that of the 42,000-ton tanker, *Pacific Glory* (see fig. 73), which collided with the 77,000-ton *Allegro*. The collision occurred off the Isle of Wight on 24 October 1979. There was an explosion in the engine room of the *Pacific Glory*, and 14 lives were lost. It was later discovered that a number of officers on both ships did not have the correct certificates.

Another example where the crew were equally culpable was when the oil carrying *Atlantic Empress* was in collision with another VLCC (Very Large Cargo Carrier), the *Aegean Captain*, off Tobago on 19 July 1979. The *Atlantic Empress* caught fire and sank with heavy loss of life and the loss of 270,000 tons of crude oil valued at $45 million. It transpired that radar had been used incompetently by the watchkeepers aboard both ships, that the watchkeeping officer on the *Atlantic Empress* at the time of the collision had been the ship's radio officer and that her master's navigation had been hopelessly inaccurate.

Not only are officers aboard f-o-c ships sometimes unqualified but they and their crews are inadequately trained. The Captain of the *Atlantic Empress* had never held a boat drill at sea during the 10 months he had been aboard, and the mishandling of a lifeboat led to the drowning of 26 of his crew.

Unpreventable disasters

Of course, not all disasters at sea can by put down to f-o-c ships, or the fallibility of a crew, marine architects or owners (though it is estimated that 70 per cent of all maritime casualties are caused by human error). Bad weather, fire, shifting cargo, mechanical breakdown – and, of course, war – all contribute to the continuing toll on shipping. Negligence may be a contributory factor when these hazards strike, but even if seamen were perfect there would still be disaster. However, it has been suggested that even in the most carefully run company seamen are not as efficient as they might be simply because in today's ships the sea itself is no longer such a direct threat. When a vessel is automated to the extent that most now are it must be difficult, or so the argument runs, for the crew to remain alert.

This visual record of maritime disasters in and around British waters will, I hope, act as a reminder that our economy still relies to a degree on those who choose to earn their living by going to sea, and that the ships seamen serve in are not always as safe as they might be. This safety factor concerns us all, not only because of the potential loss of life which might occur, but also because the pollution caused by an accident like the *Amoco Cadiz* has a direct, and adverse, effect on the environment which so many people are working hard to preserve for future generations.

1. An early unknown wreck on Cromer beach *(RNLI)*

Shipwreck!

2. An early example of what happens when a Captain tries to take a short-cut: the paddle steamer, *Earl of Arran*, aground on Nornour in the Scillies, July 1872, after striking a rock. The Captain of the Penzance – Scilly packet had been persuaded by a passenger to shorten his usual route, with disastrous results. Everyone was saved but the *Earl of Arran* was a total loss *(Gibson)*

Shipwreck!

3. The Dutch brigantine, *Catherina*, bound for Riga from Runcorn with a cargo of salt, proved to be a great attraction to the locals when she was stranded on Llandudno beach in 1869 *(Gwynedd County Council)*

4. The *Queen*, wrecked on Aberdeen beach, 1873 *(Aberdeen Library)*

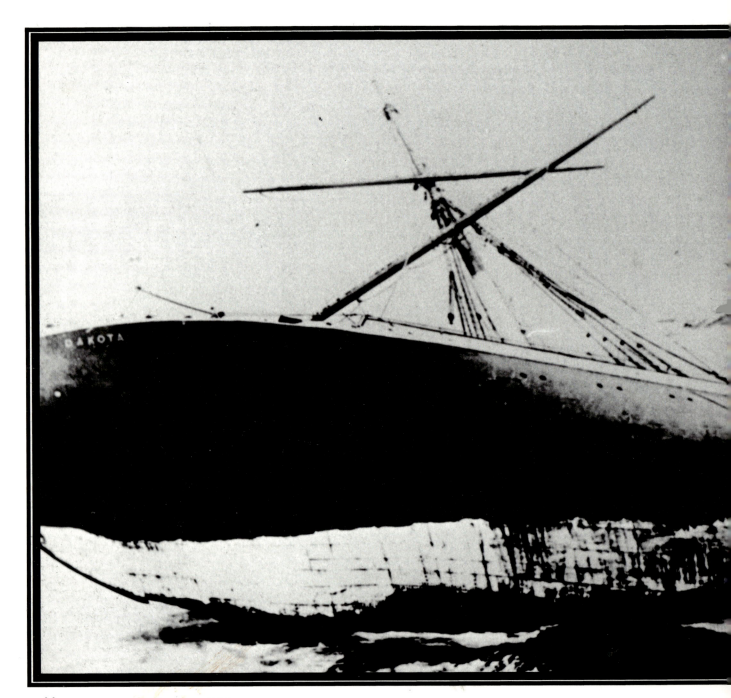

5. Human error wrecked the 4332-ton passenger steamer, *Dakota* off Amlwch, North Wales. on 9 March 1877. While on passage from Liverpool to America with 218 passengers and 109 crew aboard, the helmsman was ordered to port his helm. Instead he put it to starboard and ran her aground. Everyone aboard was saved, but the ship broke in two the following day and became a total wreck *(Gwynedd County Council)*

6. The appalling consequences of a maritime collision: the remains of the 251-ton iron-built pleasure paddle steamer, *Princess Alice*, after she had been sunk on the Thames on 3 September 1878 with the loss of over 600 lives. She was returning from Sheerness to Woolwich and was proceeding at her top speed, 11 knots, and keeping to the south bank, when the 1370-ton steamer, *Bywell Castle*, approaching from the opposite direction, rammed and sank her. Inadequate collision regulations were partly to blame for this disaster *(London Borough of Greenwich)*

7. In March 1878 the 921-ton training frigate HMS *Eurydice* capsized in a driving blizzard off the Isle of Wight. Only two out of the crew of 366 were saved. It was rumoured that the entire crew had been drinking at the end of what had been a long voyage from the West Indies. Certainly the Captain had failed to take even the most elementary precautions against bad weather, and when a black squall hit the frigate her gunports were still open and her sails unreefed. She sank in 11 fathoms but was later raised and her remains, seen in this photograph, were beached on Bembridge Ledge *(Isle of Wight Council)*

8. An early Cunard liner, the 774-ton *Balbec*, sinking in Nanjizal Bay near Land's End. The *Balbec* was on her way to Le Havre from Liverpool with a general cargo and five passengers aboard when she struck a submerged object near the Longships and started to sink. The Captain ran her aground, and her passengers and crew of 29 all landed safely in the ship's boats *(Gibson)*

9. Trippers aboard the paddle steamer *Bournemouth* had an unexpected ending to their day outing to Torquay on 27 August 1886 when, in dense fog, she ran aground on Portland Bill. Luckily, the weather was calm and all 180 passengers and 14 crew were saved *(Weymouth Museum)*

10 and 11. A victim of fog in the English Channel: the wreck of 2225-ton *Cormorant* at Ladder Chine, Chale Bay, on the Isle of Wight, December 1886 during salvage operations. She was carrying a cargo of cotton bales from New Orleans to Bremen when she ran into dense fog which reduced visibility to 50 yards. The Captain altered course to the north to try and get a bearing from the land but neither reduced his speed nor tried to take a sounding, and she ran aground. Bad luck and bad weather prevented her from being refloated and she became a total wreck *(Isle of Wight Council)*

11. See previous page

12. Locals posing by the remains of the Deal pilot lugger, *Pride of the Sea*, which was driven ashore and wrecked in Luccombe Bay on 29 October 1887 *(Isle of Wight Council)*

13. Fog has always been one of the worst hazards facing a mariner at sea. Here is one of its early victims, the *Castleford*, which ran aground on one of the Isles of Scilly in thick weather on 8 June 1887. She was carrying 450 head of cattle, most of which were saved. Note that steamers in those days still carried sails as a secondary means of propulsion *(Gibson)*

14. On 17 May 1888 the *Jean Hortense* was driven ashore during heavy weather near St Michael's Mount, which can be seen in the background. The Penzance lifeboat, which had been drawn to the scene of the incident by the carriage in the foreground, is bringing ashore the ship's crew. The brigantine was later refloated *(RNLI)*

15. While carrying timber from Sweden to Dieppe, the Le Havre barque, *Vausan*, ran into heavy weather in the North Sea and was driven ashore near Great Yarmouth on 4 November 1888. She was towed off but became a total loss *(Norfolk Museums' Service)*

16. A dramatic photograph of the West Highland passenger steamer, *Mountaineer*, which ran aground in thick fog at Oban on 27 September 1889. All her passengers and crew were saved, but the following month she broke in two and became a total loss *(University of Glasgow)*

17. A rare maritime disaster. The 2347-ton *Irex* was a brand new ship when she was driven ashore under the 400ft cliffs of Scratchells Bay on the south side of the Isle of Wight by her Captain. She set sail for Rio de Janeiro from Greenock on 10 December 1889 with a cargo of over 3500 tons of iron and earthenware and almost immediately ran into bad weather. For more than 10 days she was battered by hurricane-force winds in the Bay of Biscay before running for shelter at Falmouth. However, the weather was so bad that no pilot would come out to

18. The 2244-ton *Malta*, a liner belonging to the Cunard Line, was on her way to Genoa from Liverpool with 19 passengers and a general cargo when she ran aground in thick fog near Cape Cornwall on 15 October 1889. All her passengers and crew were saved, but the *Malta* became a complete wreck. This photograph shows local boats hugging close to the sinking ship waiting for anything valuable to float to the surface from her broken holds *(Gibson)*

her, and the exhausted Captain and crew were forced to raise sail once more and keep heading east. By now, the Captain had not been to bed for 24 days and when in sight of the Needle's Light – which he took to be that of a pilot boat – he began to hallucinate. He ordered the ship to head for the light and sent her to her doom. The Captain and six of his crew died, and the survivors were eventually rescued by rocket apparatus after climbing into the rigging away from the wave-swept decks *(Blackgang Chine Museum)*

Shipwreck!

19. The wreck of the *Evviva* which was driven ashore in Fishguard Bay in November 1893 *(Goddard)*

20. The French brigantine, *ACL*, which went ashore at Woolacombe Sands, North Devon, in January 1893
(Ilfracombe Museum)

21. The steamer *Rowan*, which went aground at Redcar on 14 April 1893 *(Redcar Library)*

22. The 129-ton schooner, *Lizzie R. Wilce*, in Ilfracombe Harbour, North Devon, after she had collided with the steamer *Yesso* in the Bristol Channel in March 1894. Three lives were lost. The schooner was obviously an unlucky ship because in 1908, as fig. 37 shows, she was driven ashore in a gale and became a total loss *(Ilfracombe Museum)*

23. The 70-ton *Arabella* after she had been wrecked on Britton's Rock, Ilfracombe, on 2 October 1895. All the crew were drowned *(Ilfracombe Museum)*

Shipwreck!

24. The stylized beauty of this photograph makes it hard to realize that it depicts the dying hours of an elegant windjammer. The *Granite State* was carrying wheat from Falmouth to Swansea in November 1895 when her Mate made a navigational error and she struck the notorious Runnel Stone, three miles south-east of Land's End. She was towed to Porthcurno Bay, where this picture was taken, but could not be saved and was later completely destroyed by a gale *(Gibson)*

25. The excursion steamer, *Davaar*, aground on the rocks at Groomsport, Co. Down in 1895 *(Ulster Museum)*

26. The barque, *Sarah*, wrecked on Great Yarmouth beach, 1899 *(Norfolk Museums' Service)*

27. Another extraordinary example of bad navigation. In the middle of the night of 9 December 1898, the Mate of the tramp *Blue Jacket* put his ship aground right under the Longships lighthouse. Visibility at the time was at least two miles, and the lighthouse must have been plainly seen by the Mate. Perhaps he just didn't bother to look *(Gibson)*

Shipwreck!

28. Violent squalls and driving rain drove the German 1300-ton barque, *Auguste*, off course as she was sailing down the English Channel on 15 February 1900 bound for Australia from London. In the reduced visibility the Captain was unable to see the danger he was in until it was too late, and she ran onto Atherfield Ledge on the south side of the Isle of Wight. In the dramatic rescue that followed, the local lifeboat rescued all 18 crew, who had taken to the rigging, but their ship could not be salvaged and later broke up *(Blackgang Chine Museum)*

29. Sailing vessels driven ashore onto the Goodwick Sands, Pembrokeshire, during a storm in the early 1900s *(Goddard)*

Shipwreck!

30. The Dutch trading barquentine, *Voorspoed*, was a victim of the weather when she was driven ashore in Perran Bay on 7 March 1901 by a northerly gale. The crew was brought safely ashore by breeches buoys but most of her cargo was looted by local people. The Captain later announced that though he had been shipwrecked all over the world he had never encountered such savages as those who inhabited Perranporth. However, the crowds in this photograph are just interested spectators as there were three policemen on board to prevent any further pilfering. The *Voorspoed* was eventually refloated, but during her next voyage, to Newfoundland, she went down with all hands *(Gibson)*

31. The steamer *Dinnington* stranded on Portland breakwater during a gale in March 1901. She was later refloated and there was no loss of life *(Weymouth Museum)*

32. Whisky Galore! The *Stewart* was bound from Liverpool to New Zealand when, on the night of 6 April 1901, she ran aground at Porth Ty Mawr, Penllech, Wales, scattering her cargo of whisky far and wide *(Gwynedd County Council)*

33. The *Glenbervie* was carrying a cargo of liquor and grand pianos when she struck the Manacles in December 1901. She then went aground near Lowland Point, and the crew were taken off by the Coverack lifeboat. The liquor was saved, but the pianos were ruined *(Gibson)*

34. Another ship to fall foul of the rugged coast of the southern side of the Isle of Wight was the brig, *Russie*. However, she was not a victim of too much wind but of too little – and of a careless crew. On Easter Sunday 1902 she was outward bound for Newfoundland when she was steered too close to the shore off St Catherine's. The fickle wind died, and she drifted on to Rocken End. None of the crew was lost, but the ship was soon smashed to pieces. Though apparently loaded only with fishing gear and salt it became obvious, once she began to break up, that she was really smuggling wine and spirits. Barrels of it floated ashore, and the locals were soon enjoying such an orgy of drinking that they reportedly, 'just fell and lay about anywhere in a state of oblivion' *(Blackgang Chine Museum)*

35. On 9 November 1902 the 170-ton three-masted schooner, *Maggie Williams* of Barrow, was making for Yarmouth harbour in strong winds when she missed stays and was swept into Gorleston breakwater and wrecked. The crew of seven were saved *(Norfolk Museums' Service)*

Shipwreck!

36. Wreck of the steamer, *James Hall*, off Aberdeen, 1903
(Aberdeen Library)

37. These two trading schooners stranded almost simultaneously on Porthminster Beach during a gale on 7 January 1908. The *Mary Barrow*, furthest from the camera, was refloated but the *Lizzie R. Wilce* never sailed again *(Gibson)*

Shipwreck!

38. A dramatic photograph of the sinking steamship, *Isle of Iona*, wrecked off Whitby during a storm on 7 December 1909. Part of Whitby Pier can be seen on the right of the picture *(Redcar Library)*

39. This unusual photograph shows the 12,500-ton liner, *Suevic*, at the beginning of her tow to Southampton after losing her bow close to the Lizard on 17 March 1907. She was near the finish of her voyage from Australia with 456 passengers and crew aboard when a combination of bad navigation and bad visibility put her on the Maenheere Rock. The passengers and crew were all rescued by the RNLI, its single biggest life-saving operation ever, but the *Suevic* later broke in two. However, a new bow was fitted and the liner had a long and useful life before being scuttled in 1942 by her Norwegian crew to prevent her falling into the hands of the Germans *(Gibson)*

40. The Norwegian barque, *Ceres*, after being driven ashore on Scroby Sand near Great Yarmouth in October 1910. All her crew were rescued by the local lifeboat, but she broke up soon afterwards *(Norfolk Museums' Service)*

41. The 5081-ton five-masted German schooner, *Preussen*, was the largest sailing ship in the world at the time she was wrecked. On the night of 4 November 1910 she ran into a severe gale in the English Channel and on 6 November she collided with another vessel losing her jib-boom and springing a leak forward. That evening she anchored off Dungeness but her cables parted and she was driven out to sea. She was taken in tow by a tug, but the tow snapped off St Margaret's Bay and she ran ashore at the foot of South Foreland Lighthouse. The crew refused to leave her and for some weeks worked to free her. But in January another broke her in half, and she had to be abandoned *(Deal Library)*

42. A victim of the Goodwins: the 5730-ton freighter, *Mahratta*, was on a voyage from Calcutta to London when she ran aground on these treacherous sands off the Kent coast on 19 April 1909 and later broke in two (*Deal Library*)

Shipwreck!

43. Whilst on her way from Sweden to Melbourne in November 1911 the *Hansey* missed stays during a gale and was driven ashore in Hounsel Bay near the Lizard. Her crew were all saved by breeches buoy, but she lost her cargo of timber and pig-iron *(Gibson)*

44. The world's most famous maritime disaster: the 46,000-ton White Star liner, *Titanic*, leaving her builders Harland and Wolff, Belfast, for her first sea trials. She sank on 14 April 1912 after hitting an iceberg with the loss of 1503 lives *(Maxtone-Graham)*

45. The steamer, *Tripolitania*, in Mount's Bay in December 1912 after her Captain had deliberately driven her ashore at full speed through high surf to save the lives of his crew from hurricane force winds. All but one made it safely ashore, but the *Tripolitania* could not be salvaged and later broke up *(Gibson)*

46. The Norwegian three-masted barque, *Gunvor*, was bringing nitrates from South America to Falmouth when she ran into fog off the Lizard on 6 April 1912 and went aground on Black Head. She grounded so close to the rocks that the crew were able to escape down the rope ladder *(Gibson)*

47. In February 1913 the German liner, *Bulow*, was on her way to Southampton from Yokohama when she ran aground at Blacknor Point, Portland, after deviating from her course,. There were 400 passengers on board but no one was injured, and she was soon towed off, practically undamaged *(Weymouth Museum)*

48. Another victim of fog was the *Cromdale*, which ran aground at Bass Point on 23 May 1913. The crew were saved, but a gale soon broke up this handsome-looking ship *(Gibson)*

49. The Rotterdam registered steamer, *Dorothea*, stranded on Chesil Beach in Portland Bay, February 1914 *(Weymouth Museum)*

50. The fog that brought an end to the ship in this eerie photograph can be seen lingering over the land in the background. The *Mildred* struck the rocks under Gurnard's Head on 6 April 1912 while carrying slag from Newport to London *(Gibson)*

51. A helpless victim of the wreck of the *Trifolium* whose cargo shifted during a gale off the Lizard in March 1914. She was driven towards land, and five of her crew were killed or drowned. Five others managed to get ashore alive after the ship disintegrated in Whitesand Bay *(Gibson)*

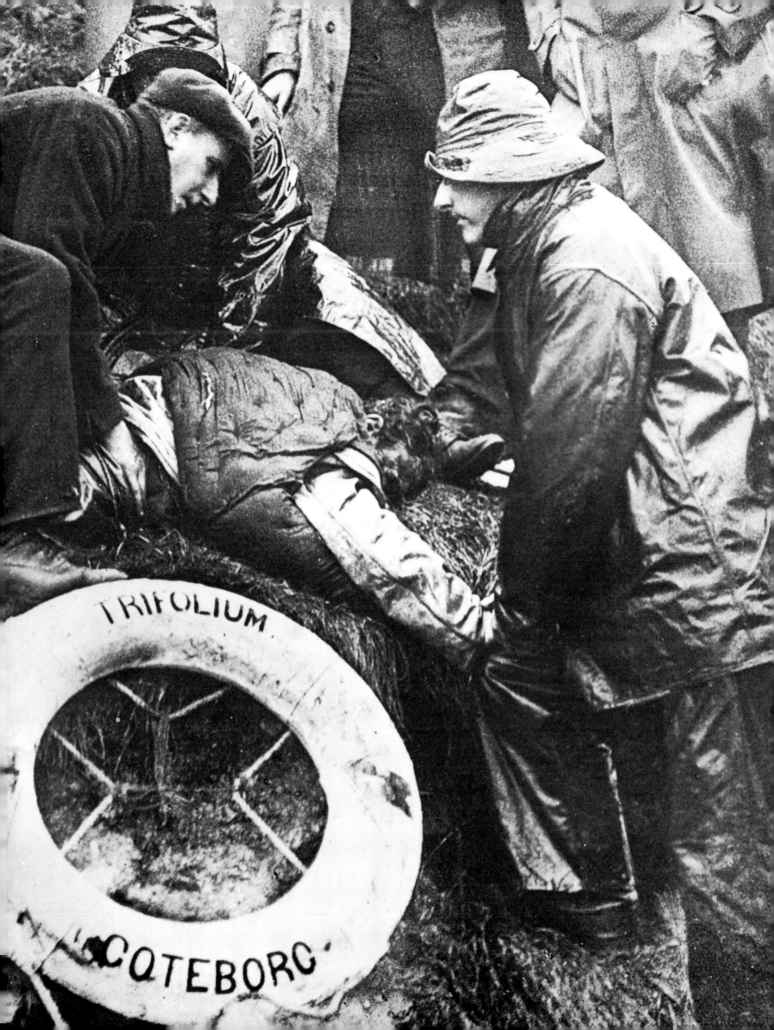

52. Curious crowds collecting round the steamer, *Lord Cecil*, which ran aground opposite the bandstand at Redcar on 12 March 1916 *(Redcar Library)*

53. On 9 January 1920 the 3226-ton freighter, *Treville*, was returning to Dundee from Calcutta with a cargo of jute and manganese when she ran aground on Kimmeridge Ledge, near Weymouth, in heavy weather. The local lifeboat could not approach her, and when the Captain and crew tried to abandon her, the ship's boat overturned. Only seven of the crew of 43 survived. The tragedy was compounded when a drifter trying to salvage the cargo hit the wreck and sank. Two years later another steamer, the *Glenmore*, also hit the remains of the *Treville* and sank nearby *(Weymouth Museum)*

54. The crew of the French schooner, *Ardente*, being rescued by the local lifeboat after a gale drove her ashore in Weymouth Bay on 11 December 1914 *(Weymouth Museum)*

55. The steamship, *Princess Clementie*, beginning to break up after being stranded at Staithes on 19 November 1924 *(Redcar Library)*

56. Another victim of Chesil Beach was a French trading vessel, *Madeleine Tristan*, which was driven ashore in September 1930. Embayed by a terrific gale, the Captain deliberately ran his ship ashore in the hope of saving his crew. He was successful in this, but his ship became a total wreck *(Weymouth Museum)*

Shipwreck!

57. Dense fog caused the Greek freighter, *Preveza*, to run ashore in Chesil Cove, Portland Bay, in January 1920. Although local tugs tried to pull her off, she remained fast and the following week began to break up *(Weymouth Museum)*

58. The *Emma* being pounded by heavy seas near Weymouth in October 1931 *(Weymouth Museum)*
59. Fire – the French liner *L'Atlantique* ablaze in the English channel in January 1933 *(Weymouth Museum)*

60. The 3111-ton Finnish barque, *Herzogin Cecilie*, had just won the Australian Grain Race for the eighth time when on the morning of 25 April 1936 she ran on to the rocks near Salcombe, Devon, in thick fog. At the time she was the largest sailing ship in Lloyds Register. No lives were lost, but after being towed into a nearby bay for repairs a gale sprang up which broke her back, and she sank *(Western Morning News)*

61. On 5 January 1947, in clear visibility and moderate seas, the 3874-ton Greek freighter, *Varvassi*, ran onto the Needles rocks at the Western end of the Isle of Wight. Her remains are still visible at low tide *(Medland Printers)*

Shipwreck!

63. The wreck of the 80-ton ketch, *Reliance*, on Portland Bill, June 1949. Her inexperienced crew had little idea of where they were and of what to do in an emergency, and when the ketch's engine failed they were driven into the cliffs. Frank Davison died in the water, but his wife Ann survived and went on to be the first woman ever to cross the Atlantic alone under sail *(Weymouth Museum)*

62. Yet another victim of fog in the English Channel: the 5000-ton Italian steamer, *Luigi Accame*, aground off Rocken End, Isle of Wight, 6 April 1937 *(Isle of Wight Council)*

Shipwreck!

64. The French railway steamer, *Agen*, in two halves after being driven on to the Goodwin Sands by a storm on the night of 13/14 January 1952. All her crew were saved *(Skyfotos)*

65. A victim of ferocious weather conditions: the South Goodwin's lightship wrecked on the very sands from which she was designed to protect Channel shipping. On the night of 26 November 1954 an 80 mph (128 kmph) gale tore her from her moorings and drove her onto Goodwin Sands, All seven of her crew were drowned, though miraculously a scientist who was also aboard survived *(Skyfotos)*

Shipwreck!

66. The crew of the 21,125-ton Liberian oil tanker, *World Concord*, being rescued by the St David's lifeboat after the tanker broke in two during a hurricane on the night of 27 November 1954 off the Pembrokeshire coast *(Goddard)*

67. The 10,788-ton Swedish tanker, *Johannishus*, on fire after colliding with a Panamanian freighter 20 miles off Margate on 9 June 1955. She burst into flames immediately and the crew were forced to jump into the water. Eighteen lost their lives *(Skyfotos)*

68. (Above) The 7142-ton coaster, *Kingsbridge*, went aground on Brighstone Ledge, Isle of Wight, on 21 January 1955, and all efforts to free her failed. Then, for the first time ever, a helicopter was used to pass a towing line between the stricken ship and a tug, and the coaster was refloated *(Isle of Wight Council)*

69. (Right) The 7176-ton Panamanian freighter, *Mando*, aground off Round Island in the Scillies. She ran into dense fog on the night of 21 January 1955. All the crew were saved by the St Mary's lifeboat, but the ship became a total loss *(Western Morning News)*

70. The coaster, *Luminence*, listing heavily after running onto the Smalls, off the Pembrokeshire coast, in March 1967. She sank soon afterwards *(Goddard)*

71. Moment of tragedy: the Fraserburgh lifeboat being overturned by a huge wave on 22 January 1970 after being launched to aid a Danish fishing vessel which was in distress. Only one lifeboatman survived. The previous year the Longhope lifeboat was lost with all hands when going to the aid of a ship which, through incompetence, had run out of fuel and was being driven ashore *(RNLI)*

72. A short cut which ended in disaster on a vast scale: the 123,000-dwt oil tanker, *Torrey Canyon*, seen here after she had run on the the notorious Seven Stones Reef between the Scillies and Land's End on 18 March 1967. She struck the reef at full speed after her Captain had decided to take a short cut to his final destination, Milford Haven. There was a massive spillage of her cargo which caused terrible pollution on both sides of the English Channel. When all efforts to salvage the ship and the remainder of her cargo proved to be of no avail, she was bombed and set alight by the RAF *(RNAS Culdrose)*

73. The 77,648-dwt oil tanker, *Pacific Glory*, on fire off the Isle of Wight, 23 October 1970. She had been on a converging course with another tanker, the *Allegro*, and avoiding action had been taken too late by the inexperienced officers aboard. The sterns of the ships collided as they steered away from each other. The *Allegro* was not seriously damaged but the bulkhead between the aft starboard tank and the

Shipwreck!

pump room in the *Pacific Glory* was fractured, and oil poured into her engine room through unsealed pump shaft openings. This caused a build up of gas which was then ignited by the diesel engine and caused an explosion in the engine room in which 14 men lost their lives. She was later beached and salvaged *(Nautical Institute)*

74. The end of the oil tanker, *Texaco Caribbean*, after colliding in the English Channel on 11 January 1971 with the Peruvian freighter, *Paracas*. The tanker exploded, killing nine of her crew and shattering windows in Folkestone five miles away. The wreck was at once marked with lights, but the following day a freighter hit it and sank. A lightship and extra buoys were added, but the following month the Greek freighter, *Nike*, hit the wreck and went to the bottom with all her crew. This disastrous series of accidents led to the introduction of a new buoyage system in the English Channel *(Skyfotos)*

75. This dramatic picture of the upturned hull of the Danish coaster, *Merc Enterprise*, which came to grief in high seas off Plymouth on 16 January 1974, shows the appalling conditions in which air-sea rescue operations often have to be carried out. It can be seen that the Sea King helicopter on the left is in the process of rescuing some of the stricken vessel's crew from their liferaft. Eight others lost their lives *(RNAS Culdrose)*

Shipwreck!

77. A modern maritime disaster: the 493-ton motor vessel, *Biscaya*, listing heavily after colliding at night with an oil rig that was being towed to the North Sea oilfields (13 December 1974). The Great Yarmouth and Gorleston lifeboat rescued the crew but the *Biscaya* sank shortly afterwards *(RNLI)*

76. The *Biscaya* (see fig. 77) *(RNLI)*

78. The brand-new 275,000-dwt oil tanker, *Olympic Bravery*, aground off the French coast, on 24 January 1976. She had been ordered before the huge rise in oil prices and was fitted with an uneconomic steam turbine engine. She ran aground soon after her owners had taken delivery of her while on her way to being laid up. She was insured for $26 million *(Nautical Institute)*

79. On 11 February 1974 the engines of the 1400-ton coaster, *Lutria*, broke down 100 miles south-west of the Lizard in high winds and heavy seas. Waves tore off the forward hold hatch covers, water poured in, and the *Lutria* began to sink. The crew took to the lifeboats and were later rescued by Sea King helicopters based at Helston in Cornwall *(RNAS Culdrose)*

80. The 1241-ton Panamanian cattle freighter, *El Tambo*, going down by the bows in Fishguard harbour in March 1977. The previous month an explosion in her engine room had ripped a hole in her side, and it took the authorities two weeks to arrange for the transfer of the cattle aboard her. Shortly afterwards she foundered during a gale *(Goddard)*

81. Air-sea rescue operations during a modern maritime disaster. Storm-force 10 winds in the English Channel in February 1978 snapped the towing line between the German tug, *Seefalke*, and the oil rig *Orion* which was being delivered to Brazil from Rotterdam. The *Orion*, with 33 crewman aboard, was driven hopelessly towards the Guernsey coast. Two of the crewmen were rescued by the St Peter Port lifeboat in a remarkable feat of seamanship, but the rig then ran aground. Two Sea King helicopters from RNAS Culdrose were

Shipwreck!

scrambled and, by carefully avoiding the 290-ft legs as they hovered, took off all but two of the crew, who were rescued by breeches buoy *(RNAS Culdrose)*

82. (main picture) The ro-ro vessel, *Hero*, carrying a cargo valued at $3 million, was abandoned in heavy weather in the North Sea on 12 November 1977 after she began to take in water. She sank 28 hours later. One man lost his life *(Canadian Forces Photo)*

83. Lack of basic navigational skills put the oil tanker, *Christol Bitas*, onto the Hats and Barrels rocks off the Pembrokeshire coast on 12 October 1978. When her hull was found to be leaking, threatening oil pollution in Cardigan Bay, her cargo was transferred. Alongside the crippled vessel is the tanker, *Esso York (Goddard)*

84. Pollution, a modern maritime hazard. Seen here are the remains of the 23,000-ton oil tanker, *Amoco Cadiz*, which ran aground near Brest on 16 March 1978. Her steering gear failed as she was entering the English Channel and she was adrift for 11 hours before being taken in tow by a tug. During this time she failed to advise either the British or the French authorities of her plight. Though the tug was quite unable to cope, the tanker's Master apparently thought that it could. Consequently, he failed to anchor at slack water and only tried to do so after the tow rope broke. By then, however, it was too late; his ship went on to the rocks and the resultant oil slick caused utter devastation to that part of the French coastline *(RNAS Culdrose)*

Shipwreck!

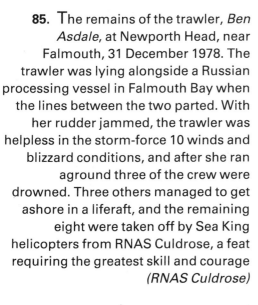

85. The remains of the trawler, *Ben Asdale*, at Newporth Head, near Falmouth, 31 December 1978. The trawler was lying alongside a Russian processing vessel in Falmouth Bay when the lines between the two parted. With her rudder jammed, the trawler was helpless in the storm-force 10 winds and blizzard conditions, and after she ran aground three of the crew were drowned. Three others managed to get ashore in a liferaft, and the remaining eight were taken off by Sea King helicopters from RNAS Culdrose, a feat requiring the greatest skill and courage *(RNAS Culdrose)*

86. There is an old saying in the Merchant Navy – Don't leave the ship until the ship leaves you – which was not observed by the Captain of this super-tanker, the *Andros Patria*, seen here being aided by a Wijsmuller tug after an explosion had ripped through a midship tank on the port side. She was off the north-west coast of Spain on 31 December 1978 when the accident occurred. The Captain thought the fire was in danger of spreading and, ignoring the high seas that were running, ordered the crew to launch a lifeboat. All but two of the crew obeyed, but the heavy seas overturned the lifeboat and everyone in it was drowned. The Chief Engineer and one of the crew had refused to go into the lifeboat and they restarted the engines and set the autohelm on a course away from the coast *(Nautical Institute)*

87. The 121,430 dwt tanker, *Betelguese*, was unloading her cargo at the oil terminal in Bantry Bay on 8 January 1979 when she blew up and sank. Fifty people died. When salvaged it was discovered that she was in an extremely wasted condition and was not fit to be at sea. An inquiry launched by the Irish government concluded that the explosion had probably been caused by the buckling of wasted longitudinals while unloading without the use of inert gas *(Nautical Institute)*

88. The 999-ton West German freighter, *Tarpenbek*, was carrying 1500 tons of lubricating oil when she collided with a Fleet Auxiliary vessel off the Sussex coast on 21 June 1979. While efforts were being made to avoid yet another pollution crisis by transferring her cargo, a storm off Selsey Bill capsized her. However, she was eventually towed into Sandown Bay where, despite the protests of anxious residents, her cargo was pumped out safely and the vessel righted. No pollution occurred, and the residents threw a party for the salvagers *(Nautical Institute)*

89. A Wessex V helicopter form RNAS Culdrose hovering above the English yacht, *Camargue*, during the 1979 Fastnet Race. Storm-force 10 winds shipped up huge, steep seas which overwhelmed a number of the smaller competitors, and 24 yachts were abandoned, some in sinking condition. Fifteen yachtsmen died *(RNAS Culdrose)*

90. The 2774-ton Greek owned freighter, *Skopelos Sky*, almost submerged by the waves after being driven ashore on the Cornish coast by hurricane force winds on 16 December 1979. All her crew were rescued by helicopter *(RNAS Culdrose)*

＊ TATER DHU

91. The upturned hull of the coaster, *Union Star*, which came to grief half a mile from the Tater＊ Light in Cornwall on 19 December 1981. Despite gale warnings, the ship's crew apparently elected to remain close to the lee shore and were subsequently driven on to it when their engine failed. This in turn led to the loss of the crew of the Penlee lifeboat, which had gone out to rescue those aboard the *Union Star*, for all lost their lives when the lifeboat overturned *(RNAS Culdrose)*

Shipwreck!

92. The rear half of the 28,572-dwt tanker, *Tanio*, being towed into mid-Channel by a French tug. She broke in half in heavy weather off the Northern coast of Brittany in March 1980 with the loss of four of her crew. She was built as long ago as 1958 and, according to one of her former Captains, she was a 'floating derelict' and eaten with rust. Though she was carrying 13,000 tons of very heavy fuel oil, luckily not more that 6000 tons leaked out. Even so $18 million had to be paid out in compensation for the pollution caused *(Nautical Institute)*

93. The *Marina di Equa* on the point of foundering in the Bay of Biscay, 29 December 1981. This 32,818-dwt bulk carrier was carrying steel products when, in heavy weather, water began coming in through No 1 hatch. She radioed for assistance, and this photograph was taken by an air-sea rescue helicopter. The helicopter was forced to return to base to refuel and when it returned, the carrier had disappeared with the loss of all hands aboard. Only some empty liferafts were found. An inquiry held by the Italian government concluded that when the No 1 hold had filled with water, the bulkhead between it and the No 2 hold must have given way, and the bulk carrier would then have sunk immediately. The *Marina di Equa* is one of a long list of bulk carriers carrying steel, scrap or iron ore which have foundered in bad weather *(Nautical Institute)*

94 (below). Another case of premature abandonment occurred when the 21,032-dwt molasses tanker, *Victory*, broke in half in the Atlantic in February 1982. Though they had not been given any order to do so, the Chief Engineer and 12 of the crew abandoned ship after deciding it was too dangerous to stay on board. However, the sea was very rough, the lifeboat overturned, and all aboard it were drowned. Ironically, the stern half, seen here, remained afloat for another two weeks and the rest of the crew were rescued by helicopter. Apparently, the *Victory* had been loaded in a way that would reduce cleaning costs, but this resulted in overstressing that caused her to break in half. Two years later a similar molasses tanker, the *Tesubu II*, was lost with all hands in the Indian Ocean
(Nautical Institute)

95. Another ro-ro ferry disaster occurred in August 1985 when the *Mont Louis* collided with the *Olau Britannia* off the Belgian coast and turned on her side. It was very nearly a pollution disaster, too, for the ferry was carrying a highly radioactive cargo of uranium hexafluoride. As can be seen here, a hole had to be cut in her side to remove it *(Fotoflite)*

96. On 21 December 1982 the 4263-ton ro-ro ferry, *European Gateway*, was in collision with another ferry outside Felixstowe harbour. She overturned and sank in 20 feet of water, and six men died. She is seen in this picture being righted by the Wijsmuller salvage vessel, *Super Servant 3 (Wijsmuller)*

97. Swift action on the part of the Dutch salvage company, Smit Tak, saved the North Sea marine environment from disaster after the 3555-ton *Olaf* capsized off the Dutch coast in July 1986. She carried a cargo of highly pollutant material which had to be raised immediately, and in the photograph the ship can be seen being brought to the surface by the company's specialized lifting equipment. Although North European waters are the most closely regulated in the world, shipping accidents continue to occur with alarming frequency. In the North Sea, Smit Tak alone has dealt with four major casualties over the past two years *(Smit Tak)*

98 and 99. On 6 March 1987 the 8000-ton ro-ro ferry, *Herald of Free Enterprise*, left Zeebrugge harbour bound for Dover with about 1300 passengers aboard. Though strictly against company rules, it was not unusual, in order to save time, for a ferry to leave the quayside with her bow doors still open, these being closed as the ferry proceeded out of harbour. On this occasion the bows of the *Herald of Free Enterprise* had been lowered by water ballast to compensate for the low tide at loading time and had not been adjusted when she left the quay. The crew member responsible for closing the doors did not do so, and the ship's command system failed to discover this error. This disastrous combination of mistakes resulted in the ferry shipping water into the open space of the car deck, and the vessel capsized with the loss of 193 lives. These grim photographs show the ferry capsized onto her port side, and the immensely complicated operation mounted by Smit Tak which resulted in her being raised *(Smit Tak)*

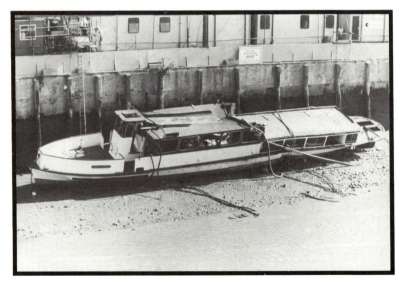

100. The battered remains of the pleasure boat, *Marchioness*, after she had been raised from the bed of the Thames. In the early hours of 20 August 1989 the 90-ton *Marchioness*, which had been hired for a birthday party, had just passed under Southwark Bridge when she was run down from astern by the 1475-ton sand dredger, *Bowbell*. 51 lives were lost.

101. Luckily this accident did not occur anywhere near the British coastline. But this photograph of the 271,540-ton Spanish crude oil carrier, *Castillo de Bellver*, on fire off the west coast of South Africa, on 6 August 1983, is a horrific final reminder of the type of marine disaster which can happen anywhere at any time. She was fully loaded with a quarter of a million tons of crude oil which gushed into the sea after she blew up. The explosion probably occurred because oil leaked into one of her huge ballast tanks and caused a build up of gas. One of the crew was killed, and it is possible that he had caused a spark while inspecting the empty tank *(Nautical Institute)*